HOW TO GET SPONSORSHIPS AND ENDORSEMENTS

Get Funding for Bands, Non-Profits, Fundraising Events, and More!

SIMON S. TAM

DEDICATION

This book is dedicated to the innumerable artists, development staff, volunteers, fundraisers, and aspiring marketers of the world who are taking great causes to heights with their efforts.

I know it's tough out there and we'd all rather just accept free checks but as Jonas Silk writes, "The reward for work well done is the opportunity to do more." Here's to your sponsorship efforts – I hope this book will help lead you to do more than you ever dreamed of.

CONTENTS

ACKNOWLEDGMENTS

I'd like to thank Allen Diaz and Lauren Knowles for encouraging me to put my thoughts to paper and publish. You've both inspired me to continue pushing the boundaries in so many different ways.

I'd also like to thank some of the people who've helped me with the revisions: Dan Crowdus (of the Icarus Kid) and Andrew Morse (of Await Rescue). Your feedback was greatly appreciated.

There have been some incredible organizations along the way who have also helped me refine the sponsorship process, including the American Cancer Society, Asian Pacific American Network of Oregon, and In the Light Ministries. The staff and volunteers have share the importance of pursuing things with passion.

Finally, some of the greatest brand partners that I've had who taught me that sponsorship was more than a simple transaction: Dewey Weddington at SakeOne, Michael Schulz and Billy Siegle at Fender, Luis Palau at Printing Conexions, fashion designer Rachel Park, Al Dickson from Red Bull…thank you for your friendship and excitement in helping my brands/causes.

1 INTRODUCTION

The first sponsorship proposal that I ever created was at the age of eleven. I was in the 7th grade. My friends and I had just created a team to compete at our school's Ultimate Frisbee competition. I didn't really know what I was doing. This was before the Internet was widely used (or personal computers for that matter) and the school library didn't have anything on the subject so there weren't any resources that I could have access to. So what did I do?

First, I made a list of what we wanted to get for our team: gloves, jerseys, and Frisbees. Second, I thought about people who might be able to provide money or products for us: the local radio station, clothing companies, Wham-O (our favorite flying disc), etc. After that, I typed up a letter and mailed it to the corporate offices of each respective company.

While that experience didn't result in our team getting the cool jerseys that we were hoping for, I did end up getting some free concert tickets (courtesy of 91.1FM) and a valuable lesson about getting sponsorships. It was never about our team and what an organization could do for us. It was all about what a sponsorship meant for their business and how working together could benefit them. I had to convince and prove to them that there would be a great Return on Investment (ROI), not just a worthwhile cause.

Several years later, I had another chance to apply those lessons. When I was junior in High School, I started the first ever, school-wide Battle of the Bands. The event served as a fundraiser for one of the school clubs where I was an officer. This became the largest fundraising event at our school and it required me to hire professional security to control the crowd size, rent an arena level sound system, and manage a volunteer group of 40 individuals. Since I was only fifteen, I had to convince my friends' older siblings to sign off on the waiver forms for me. But more importantly, we had sponsorship partners! By walking door to door in our community and explaining how they could benefit from supporting our event, I was able to get participation from over a dozen businesses.

Since then, I've helped raise hundreds of thousands of dollars through sponsorship money for fundraising events, musicians, non-profit organizations, budding businesses, and other great causes.

This book is a collection of ideas that I've learned over the years. Everything is written in an easy, step-by-step manner so that you can pick it up anytime to get advice directly related to your step in the sponsorship process. Everything that is in this book has been implemented in my own personal sponsorship efforts.

The more that I do this, the more that I realize that finding a sponsor is really about building a long-term partnership with another brand. Getting a nice check is just the tip of the iceberg for what a quality sponsorship program can provide for you. My non-profit partners have provided thousands of incredible lifelong volunteers. Sponsors who have supported my music have given me priceless memories touring the world.

I hope that this book will inspire you in your sponsorship efforts and help your artistic or charitable endeavors.

Simon Tam
May 2012

2 RETHINKING SPONSORSHIPS

When most people who want sponsorships think about their ultimate goal, it involves money. They're looking for someone to fund their event, to pay for their tour, to raise money for their charity, and so on. When many business think about sponsoring someone, it ultimately involves money as well: even if it is an incredible cause, at the end of the day, they want to know how sponsoring will help them get more customers. Each party treats the sponsorship as a transaction. However, I believe it is important to shift the definition from "a cash and/or in-kind fee paid to a property (typically sports entertainment, non-profit event, or organization) in return for access to the exploitable, commercial potential associated with that property" (IEG, 2000) to something more equitable: a partnership.

Sponsorship as a Partnership

A sponsorship insinuates something more akin to a one-sided relationship: the sponsor gives money in the hope for more customers or being associated with a positive cause. A partnership denotes an agreement where both parties share the risks, responsibilities, and rewards. By approaching the relationship as a partnership, it also implies a long term agreement.

By examining how we approach sponsorships more closely, we can also identify a few other important factors that should be considered:

- **Who do we want associated with our brand, event, or organization?** You hear about companies dropping their advertising dollars or sponsorships of athletes all the time because they don't want to be affiliated with improper behavior. Recently, talk show host Rush Limbaugh lost multiple major advertisers due to some of his controversial statements. However, sometimes as an artist or non-profit event, we don't think deeply about who we are getting our money from and how our customers' perception of us might change as a result.
- **What kind of people do we want to work with?** If you are planning a cross-promotional marketing campaign where you work closely with a brand, you'll want to know their customers, their work-flow, communication processes, and their approach. Does it make sense for what you are doing?
- **Is everyone getting fair value for their work?** If you are getting a $20,000 sponsorship, are you providing *at least* $20,000 worth of deliverable returns back to the investor? Conversely, is the amount of work you're doing worth the money/partnership or are there other ways you can get the same resources more easily?
- **What are some creative ways that this partnership can be highlighted?** You should be able to do more than simply trade logos on websites and your printed materials. How can you use your respective brands to drive customers towards one another? Is there a way that you can involve the employees of a sponsoring business?

Sales guru Jeffrey Gitomer puts it best: "All things being equal, people want to do business with their friends. All things being not so equal, people still want to do business with their friends." By elevating the value of sponsorship to an established, friendly partnership, you'll instill loyalty, and get more in return than a simple check could ever provide.

Sponsorships, Partnerships, and Endorsements: What's the Difference?

Before approaching someone for a sponsorship, it's important to understand the terms. I talk to artists on a regular basis who don't understand the nature of sponsorships, endorsements, and what the difference is between the two.

An Endorsement is...
- A recommendation of a product or service.
- Can a testimonial about a person, event, or product
- Is an approval
- May or may not be reciprocal
- Is not dependent on money (although it can involve money if it is a paid endorsement)

For example, Slash endorses Gibson Guitars: he uses them on stage and in recordings, they feature him in advertisements, and he talks about how he loves the product. Gibson Guitars does not endorse Slash. They sponsor him by providing him with cash and/or in-kind products. As a musician, it wouldn't make sense to ask for an endorsement from a music instrument company. On the other hand, if you were a high-profile musician, you could offer an endorsement to the music instrument company either because you wanted to get paid for that service (in other words, a sponsorship), or because you genuinely love their products and want others to know about the company.

In this sense, a celebrity can also endorse a charity or event they're passionate about. For instance, Michael J. Fox endorsed (and founded) the Michael J. Fox Foundation for Parkinson's Research. He used his star power in order to draw more attention to the cause and by doing so, was publicly establishing his support of the cause. It wouldn't make sense for a charity event to endorse a celebrity, would it?

An example of a one-sided endorsement would be a political endorsement or someone promoting a product simply because they love it. For instance, when Consumer Reports recommends their "best value cars," they are endorsing those vehicles.

A Traditional Sponsorship...

- Is an exchange between two brands, where one (Brand A) pays the other (Brand B) in order to be associated with the other party.
- Is where one party acts as the benefactor (the one providing products or cash) and the other is being supported through the sponsorship.
- May or may not involve a testimonial or recommendation (although one is often implied)
- May be limited by a specific term (often through a limited contract)

An example of a traditional sponsorship is the PGA Tour FedEx Cup. As the presenting sponsor, FedEx is entitled to naming rights for a major portion of the largest professional golf tournaments in the world, The PGA Tour. FedEx gives over $35 million per year to have their brand associated with the PGA Tour because they want to be associated with professional golfers. Unless there is a renewal of the contract, FedEx and the PGA Tour will not be associated with each other once the term expires.

A Partnership is...

- An exchange between two brands, organizations, or events where the results are shared and complimentary.
- Shares the risks, responsibilities, and rewards.
- When the brands will depend on each other to bring exponential growth in terms of their market share, outreach, and brand exposure.
- A long term relationship.
- Fueled by genuine enthusiasm by all of the parties involved.
- With a charity event, the sponsor provides both dollars and volunteers.

I'd like to demonstrate a brilliant, working partnership with a personal example. My band, The Slants, works very closely with a brand, G Sake. Rather than doing a simple logo swap and receiving a check, we've collaborated closely to design opportunities to showcase each other's brands. For example, in addition to the traditional forms of sponsorship (logos on websites and printed goods, naming rights to events, etc.), we've also helped create genuine endorsements of their products and connected our respective audiences through planned events. This included filming a behind-the-scenes video of their factory and performing at the sake brewery, creating genuine product placement opportunities (such as featuring bottles of the product in our music video), creating a website where fans can get unreleased music from the band hosted by G Sake, and more. The relationship evolved naturally and we're always recommending each other to prospective partners and customers. We're genuine fans of each other's brands and that passion carries across all of our marketing efforts.

When I was at the American Cancer Society, we especially valued business partnerships because in addition to financial support, they would encourage their customers and employees to be involved with our fundraising events as well. This created a greater sense of community between participants, the events, and the businesses.

With a successful partnership/sponsorship, the two brands are so closely tied that the customer generally associates one with the other. For example, Michael Jordan and Nike.

3 MAKING YOUR BRAND ATTRACTIVE TO SPONSORS

Before you begin flooding the email boxes of marketing directors about your music, event, or charity, be sure that you have something worth selling. In other words, before you begin pitching your idea, you better perfect your product. For the busy business owner or executive, there's nothing that is hated more than spam messages that ramble on and waste valuable time. With some careful planning, you can make the most of your asks.

Not only is it important to fine-tune how you describe your business, it is crucial to understand what your potential sponsors are looking for. The sooner that you learn how to get that across, the sooner you'll be closing sponsorship deals! Try and keep in mind that the sponsorship proposal should be treated like a sales call. For these purposes, the potential sponsor is your customer. You'll want to do everything you can to establish credibility and develop that relationship as soon as possible.

The Elevator Pitch and the Compelling Story

I've always loved this bit of advice about applying to jobs: the purpose of a resume isn't to get you a job. The purpose of a resume is to get you an interview for the job.

All too often, we're so fixed on our accomplishments, history, benefits, media attention, etc. that we forget how to capture the mission or core values in one sentence. Other times, we're so eager to grab a person's attention through the use of a flashy introduction but fizzle out during performance (many blockbuster films come to mind).

Your organization probably has a great story. Whether you have a worthwhile cause that you are fundraising for or you're an up and coming artist, you have something worth sharing. However, even the most well-developed sponsorship proposal will be overlooked and ignored if you fail to catch the prospect's attention quickly. Conversely, if you have a great elevator pitch but don't have something substantial to follow up with, then you'll lose the sale.

The Elevator Pitch

The Elevator Pitch is the quick, pithy, attention-grabbing descriptor of who you are and what you do. It's the tweet rather than the blog. It's the teaser trailer, the preview. The purpose is exactly for its namesake: if you were in an elevator ride with your prospect and only had 15-60 seconds, what would you say? What do you do to make them want to take your card and be excited about taking your call?

Here are some general tips to help you pare down your descriptor while making it as attention grabbing as possible:

- **Use standout words:** If you can claim to be the *first*, *original*, *only*, *biggest*, or *most*, then include that for your pitch. Think of it as your new motto or catchphrase.
- **How you are different than your competitors:** Explain what makes you unique. What can you claim about your organization or event that no one else can?
- **Keep the audience in mind:** Make your claim as relevant to your sponsorship prospect as possible and draw upon any correlations that you can. For example, you might have a family-friendly fishing event and would like to get a mountain bike donated from the local cycling shop to giveaway as the prize. Rather than describing yourself as the "oldest fishing tournament in town," emphasize the related aspects such as "an event enjoyed by outdoor enthusiasts," etc.

- **If you can tweet it, keep it:** Remember, the goal is to have attention grabbing-lines for each part of your proposal that leaves them wanting more.
- **Share your value:** You want to give some sense of your value to the prospect. What should they care about? Why should they care?
- **Use a pitch wizard:** 15secondpitch.com has a free tool to help you create an effective pitch and only takes a few minutes.
- **Use the Elevator Pitch for initial contact:** This is to grab attention, not to provide an in-depth lesson. It is a great conversation starter and selling point.
- **End with a specific call to action:** After describing what you do, explain what you want: a follow-up meeting or call, a large check, free products, etc.

Here's a general format that you can use (templates and examples are available in the Appendix):

1. Who you are (name, position, organization or charity event)
2. What you/your organization/event does (1-2 sentences)
3. Why you are the best/Why you are unique
4. How this is valuable to the prospect
5. Call to action

The Compelling Story

The Compelling Story is used to get an emotional response from the prospect. This is where you generate excitement or compassion. It's the history of your organization or how you affect the community. It's the page-turning biography or tale that you would hear on Paul Harvey's radio program. It's the in-depth conversation after the speed dating encounter, the keynote speech.

If you hooked your prospect with an enticing opener and they'd like more information, this is where you really are able to highlight what you do, the benefits of them getting involved, and how your partnership with their brand will benefit the two of you. Depending on the situation (such as an in-person presentation, mailing a packet, phone meeting, etc.), you'll have different amounts of time but the whole point is to keep it interesting all the way through.

Here are some tips to keep it compelling:

- **Learn how to tell a great story:** Any great presentation or story has key elements: great pacing/rhythm, has a dramatic build-up (or multiple), it engages the audience. What resonates with your customers or most enthusiastic followers the most?
- **Talk to the brain, sell to the heart:** People who are business-minded still have emotional operatives/motivations. Use hard data and facts to show why logically, it makes sense to work with you (access to a large audience, industry leader, etc.). But also include emotional reasons too: it will be fun and exciting, they can help save a life, etc.
- **Keep it as long as you need to:** Just because you could write 30 pages or spend four hours talking about what you do doesn't mean that you should. Leave them wanting more, not bored.
- **Focus on the prospect:** Just like everything else in this process, you should be focusing on the focusing on your sponsorship prospect: How does this information relate to them or their customers? Why their company and not their competitor? What can you do for them?
- **It's a telephone, not a megaphone:** If you are able to present your proposal live rather than simply sending a packet, that's even better! Use two way conversation to keep your prospect engaged, interested, and invested into the process.

For some sponsorship proposal examples, see the Appendix.

Finding Your "It Factor"

Have you ever wondered why people are drawn to certain celebrities, songs, television commercials, or other interests? The French refer to it as *je ne sais quoi*, or the indefinable quality that makes someone special. It's the "it factor."

Sales, marketing, and advertising executives call this USP, or Unique Selling Proposition. It's a term that refers to the unique features of a brand, product, or service that differentiates them in the marketplace. Being able to set yourself apart from competitors is one of the most important elements in branding and marketing. Once you figure out what the it factor is, you find a way to communicate it that resonates with your customers (and sponsorship prospects).

Discover your it factor by answering these questions:

- What are you most well-known for?
- What do you do that no else does?
- Who is your target audience?
- In other words, how can you describe yourself in one sentence in a way that explains what is truly unique about you/your product/your organization?

Sometimes your it factor isn't what you think it is. Sometimes it isn't even related to what you consider your product. For example, Jennifer Lopez is known for her rear end rather than her musical abilities.

Here are some popular ways to frame a Unique Selling Proposition:

- **The Crossroads USP:** Combining two seemingly unrelated idea and bringing them together in an interesting way., "Dolly Parton playing heavy metal" would be a unique music style.
- **The Metaphor USP:** Using an overarching metaphor to describe the brand, product, service, idea, or approach. For instance, Neiman Marcus sells luxury while Wal-Mart sells bargains.
- **The Persona-Driven USP:** Having a persona be the voice and symbol of the brand. The particular person is what sets the organization or products apart. Martha Stewart is great example of this.
- **The Exclusive USP:** Being the only source for a certain service, information, or product.

How to Connect Your It Factor to Your Sponsor

With sponsorship proposals, not only do you have to discover what your it factor is, but you also need to demonstrate how it relates to the sponsorship prospect. Some of the ways that you can do that include:

- **Show how your USP relates to theirs:** Perhaps you have a similar target audience but are in different industries or you are able to reach completely different audiences in the same industry. Maybe your products and services complement one another.
- **Emphasize why you stand out better than your competition:** If you have unique or exclusive access to a certain audience, you make a better ally.
- **Your USP gives you credibility:** By being known as the leader (or pioneer) in your field, there is greater validity for supporting you.

Demonstrating Your Niche Market

The biggest mistake that anyone can make in marketing is to try and be everything to everyone. Bill Cosby once said, "I don't know about the key to success, but the key to failure is trying to please everybody." Not only is this true for business in general, it's also true when it comes to getting sponsorships. If you try to make your sponsorship proposition appeal to everyone possible, it will be less appealing overall.

When sharing your brand, event, or idea with potential sponsors, you have it is important to:

- **Show a keen understanding of your niche market:** Who is your most enthusiastic fan? You might reach a broad audience but there are certain types of customers that resonate your brand more than anyone else.
- **How reaching your niche market would benefit the sponsor:** Who are these people and why would your sponsorship prospect be interested in them?

- **Why the sponsor needs you to reach this niche market:** How can working with you give the sponsor credibility for your most enthusiastic fans?

Your fundraising event, band, or charity might have a wide net that covers a large variety of people but the most effective way to win over a business is to show that special niche relationship. For example, a breast cancer walk might have participants of all ages, genders, racial backgrounds, income levels, etc. but the largest, most passionate audience tends to be upper-class women in their 40's. This is the niche market that their sponsors want to reach.

The Susan G. Komen Foundation takes it a step further by identifying groups of the multiple niche markets that they hit. In their sponsorship proposal, companies can choose a sponsorship package that is geared to hit specific target audiences, For instance, their sponsorship options allow you to choose between targeting participants, corporate partners, runners, cancer survivors, volunteers, the medical community, donors, and more. They've already demonstrated incredible brand exposure and leveraging their connection with specific markets to build more effective partnerships with sponsors.

Make a Connection with Every Step

Whenever you communicate with the sponsorship prospect, whether it is through a conversation or through sending printed materials, it's important to show how there is a connection with them in every step of the process. The stronger the affiliation that they feel with your brand, the greater the possibility of them partnering with you.

These are some areas that you should try to touch on:

- Any mutual friends, business contacts or networks that you share. This might also include memberships to professional organizations or the local chamber of commerce.

- How your It Factor and Compelling Story is directly related to their business and their customers.
- How your Unique Selling Proposition (USP) is connected with their USP.
- How your audience crosses over with theirs.
- Why they need you to reach your niche audience.
- Why their customers would like to see a connection with your brand and how the relationship can affect their business.
- How the partnership can benefit the business in other ways: expansion of market presence, greater customer loyalty, employee retention/satisfaction, strengthening their brand in the community, etc.
- How other organizations have benefited from working with you.
- How a sponsorship fits in with their future plans.

In conclusion, the best way to talk about *your* sponsorship cause is to include as much about *the sponsor* as possible. The more that you can show mutual benefits, the better. You want to prove a vested interest for both parties involved so that they know you'll be enthusiastic about promoting their brand. However, they also want to know that you understand their target audience, their marketing goals, and how to reach those targets.

4 KNOWING YOUR PROSPECT: SELECTING THE RIGHT COMPANIES

Finding the right sponsorship prospects to support your cause is similar to finding the right donors, fans, volunteers, or customers. It stems from a deep understanding of what your target market is and how you can reach them best. By being selective about who you target, you can spend more time and resources developing quality, likely sponsors and less time hoping that your email blasts will eventually hit the right person. Even if you are working with a tight deadline (which I cover later on), you'll still want to be methodical about who you target.

I believe that you should always begin with those who you already know, followed by those familiar with your event/organization/case, and finally picking other contacts based on a variety of criteria.

Start With Who You Know

It's always a good idea to start with your own network before reaching out to others. There are several reasons for this:

1. It's easier to secure a sponsor if there is already an existing relationship or connection.
2. Securing sponsorships early on will add credibility for your proposal to future prospects.

3. Your existing relationships can help guide you through the sponsorship process so that you'll feel more confident (and experienced) about pursuing other contacts.

4. If you have a tough time getting buy-in from your friends and allies, you'll have a much more difficult time winning others over. That's a strong indicator that you need to work on your brand and/or sponsorship proposal before moving onto other contacts.

5. Often times, we rule out contacts who are ready/willing simply because we forget that they are right there!

When you begin sorting your contacts, these are some simple steps that you should take to ensure that the right people are included:

- **Have everyone on your organization, board of directors, band members, or whoever is connected to the effort go through their contact lists:** If you have a LinkedIn account, this is even more helpful since it lists your contacts with their organizations and the positions they hold there. Check your email contacts, cell phone, Rolodex, Facebook, and so on.

- **Go through the membership directory of any membership organization that you belong to:** Include the chamber of commerce, professional networking organizations, religious groups, clubs, etc.

- **Create a spreadsheet or document that lists the names, contact information, and organizations of those individuals.** If those contacts are associated with or have close ties with other businesses, list them next to the people that you know as well.

- **Ask your close contacts for any recommendations of people they might know:** This includes trusted business contacts, other members of professional organizations, customers, friends, colleagues, etc.

- **Use built-in social media tools to see mutual connections:** Sites like Facebook and LinkedIn often have a "people you may know" function that shows your potential relationship with that individual (mutual contacts, etc.). These are prospects that might want to include as well.

- **For indirect connections, ask for an introduction through a mutual contact:** Even if your direct contacts aren't able to help by providing a sponsorship, they often will know of someone who can.

This should provide a pretty extensive initial list of those who would most likely support your organization.

Follow Up With Who Knows You

There's often a number of potential sponsors waiting for you that you don't directly know (or aware of). This could be due to write-ups, media mentions, being involved with the community, or other forms of publicity where your message carries. Businesses and individuals who know of you through reputation make a better fit than those who have no familiarity with you at all. Here are some ways to find them:

- **Conduct an extensive search engine investigation to see where you've gotten publicity:** Use multiple search engines (Google, Yahoo, DuckDuckGo, etc.) as well as Boolean logic (such as quotation marks or brackets) to aid with your research. Find out who has written about you or where you have coverage and pay attention to the readership or audiences of those sources.
- **Use web tools to find out how people are getting to your website:** Free tools such as Google Analytics can teach you how people are landing on your page, which can give you valuable clues as to what people are looking for when they find you. This is another way to discover your USP.
- **Use the power of a survey:** Ask participants on your mailing list if they'd be willing to take a survey (it helps to offer an incentive) and include questions about their businesses or if they'd be willing to help or are interested in partnering with you.
- **Check your neighborhood:** Check with neighboring businesses if you have an office/retail location or organizations of the areas you host events in. You can even begin with a soft ask or make initial contact by asking if they'd be willing to hang a poster of an upcoming event, have a place for brochures, etc.

Once you come up with this second list, find ways to nurture those relationships so that they can become direct contacts. Either way, these individuals/organizations make great potential prospects.

Finding Other Companies to Sponsor You

Often times, you'd like to contact other organizations outside of your network or immediate area (such as the corporate office of a national organization). Before you start contacting large companies, remember that they are often bombarded with requests. For instance, Red Bull gets several hundred requests for sponsorship per week. There is much more competition. On the other hand, larger companies often have a sponsorship manager to process these proposals and have more resources to give out than smaller, local businesses. The more focused you are when you are contacting companies outside of your network, the better your results will be.

Follow these guidelines for finding other companies:

- **Start with an industry, not a company:** Before you have your heart set on a specific company, you should consider what industries would be most beneficial to you. Often times, there might be several organizations that you can contact.
- **Who are your constituents interested in?** If your customers/volunteers/fans/donors/etc. all enjoy specific products, those companies would definitely be interested in reaching out to them even more. This is why understanding your niche audience and it factor are crucial!
- **What industries are your constituents involved in?** If your niche audience is composed of a specific industry (such as college students, bartenders, or doctors), look for companies who target those groups.
- **Whose customer are you?** What products/services do you already use? Often times, companies would like to reward their most loyal and enthusiastic customers. If you depend on a product or service to operate, why not see if you can get those needs met for free?

21

- **Find out who is supporting other similar events/organizations:** It helps to see which companies are open to supporting causes similar to yours. For example, Jägermeister is known for supporting touring rock bands and have a very specific application process. If you are hosting a charity auction, see who is supporting other local charity auctions. These companies might be more willing to consider your proposal since they're already involved with sponsorships. On the other hand...

- **Who is not involved with any sponsorship programs at all:** Carve your own niche of asking companies who don't have a fully developed sponsorship load. Often times, these are companies who simply haven't been asked yet. Other times, no one has been able to demonstrate the true value of a successful partnership yet. Why not be the first?

5 HOW TO BEGIN THE SPONSORSHIP CONVERSATION

Where to Begin

If you've done the preliminary work of making your brand attractive to sponsors, developing your niche market, and identifying sponsorship prospects with the most potential, then you're already off to a great start. Those steps are the foundation on which your sponsorship campaign is built. The more carefully you work each of those areas, the more effective you will be in securing sponsorships (and hopefully developing long-term partners).

Before you make a single call or send any emails out, you'll want to make sure that you are ready to follow-up with the appropriate materials. If you don't have an updated website/social media, sponsorship proposals and agreements on hand, etc. then you might lose that sponsor simply because you'll be seen as unorganized and unprofessional.

To get a great start, follow these steps:

1. Develop your branding, niche audience, and materials.
2. Create a database of potential sponsors based on existing relationships, mutual contacts, and companies that fall outside or your network but still relate to your market.
3. Prioritize the list based on who can fulfill your priority needs, who you have the most connection with (especially established

relationships), and who would be most interested in you. In other words, who you want to call first.

4. If you have multiple people working with you (such as a committee, board of directors, volunteers, staff, etc.), divide up the list by assigning those with the strongest personal connections to initiate contact.

5. Do some basic research on the companies, their industry, their customers, etc. The more that you understand what their goals are, the better. There are many great tools available online for this including: Hoover's, Duns & Bradstreet, Marketline/Datamonitor, and LinkedIn. If you have contact names, you can use LinkedIn or do some basic searches to see if you can bring up conversational points.

6. Begin contacting your list of potential sponsors based on this order. If you have a mutual connection, ask to have an introduction be made.

How to Initiate Contact

How you contact a sponsorship prospect should depend on your relationship with them. This is why it is always important to build relationships, network, and look for other opportunities to partner up with companies.

If you already know the contact...

If you have a well-established personal relationship with someone at a company, then you should be as up front as possible. Specifically ask if they have a process for sponsorship programs or co-branded marketing campaigns and what they need from you so that you can get your proposal reviewed. You might also ask for insight such as the specific information they are looking for and that would be most useful for their decision.

However, if you feel uncomfortable with the direct ask, these are some other ways to get the sponsorship conversation going:

- **See any current or past sponsorships:** If the company is known for supporting other community events, bands, etc., try asking more about those past experiences and what they liked/didn't like about other sponsorship opportunities.

- **Offer marketing ideas, especially if they are tax deductible:** Business owners are always looking for ways to expand their market presence, get exposure to new customers, and promote their products/services. If you already have some creative ideas on how you can work together, ask for an appointment to go over some of your proposals.
- **Ask if they're passionate about charity or community events:** Sometimes people will get involved with the arts, charity fundraisers, events, etc. on an individual level but not with their business. This might be a great opportunity to blend their personal passions with growing their business.

If you don't have a relationship with the contact...

Although it can be more difficult to get the on the radar of someone who you don't have a relationship with, it isn't impossible. In fact, many new sponsorships deals are closed without any prior contacts or working history.

Here's how you work around not having a direct relationship:

- **Have a mutual colleague introduce you.** Scientists at the University of Milan have determined that the average number of acquaintances separating any two people in the world is 4.74. Odds are that you can find someone who can make an appropriate introduction to your prospect. Take advantage of social media tools and online research to see who can help you make the connection.
- **Cold call.** Many sales calls, sponsorships included, are done by simple cold calling (with no warm leads). Sometimes you just have to pick up the phone, send an email, or drop off a business card and use your elevator pitch to grab their attention. Don't waste the postage mailing a packet without at least providing the personal touch.

Who You Should Contact

If you going to be pitching a sponsorship proposal, there are usually a few key people that you should get in touch with at the company. Look at a staff directory on the company's website then use search engines or LinkedIn to get contact information. If there's no specific contact listed, call the company and ask who should be contacted for sponsorships or marketing proposals. Most of the time, they'll at least provide you with a name or department to start with.

- **Sponsorship Manager or Artist Relations:** If you are contacting a larger company that is already involved with sponsorships, they probably already have a sponsorships director or manager who leads reviewing sponsorship proposals. At music instrument companies, the equivalent position/department is artist relations.

- **VP of Marketing or Director of Marketing:** If a company doesn't have a designated department for sponsorships, then the responsibility usually falls on the marketing department. Either way, you'll eventually want to be working with marketing if you'd like to plan some co-branded campaigns or more creative endeavors.

- **Brand Manager:** These are individuals in charge of the P&L (Profit and loss) of the company affected by company loyalty. Pitching a sponsorship idea that can lift a company's reputation with their target audiences would definitely be of interest.

- **Director of Sales:** Some companies combine sales and marketing into one department. In these instances, a sales executive or manager might be interested in hearing proposals that could expand their customer base.

- **Business Owner:** With most smaller, family-owned, local businesses, the buck stops here. They're always interested in finding new ways to grow their business but might be more reluctant of financial risks, especially when there isn't a clear return on investment. Often times though, if you have larger companies already supporting you, the business owner will be more interested.

How to get contact information...

It is important to get your information directly into the hands of the decision maker so that you aren't brushed off by a gatekeeper. However, many companies are reluctant to publish direct contact information (especially for executive staff) because of the overwhelming about of spam being sent, sponsorships proposals included. If you don't know where to start, try using these tactics:

- Start with the "About" page of a company website and see if they have a staff director, staff bio's, or staff listing.
- Use a company researching tool such as:
    - Hoover's (hoovers.com)
    - OneSource Business Info (onesource.com),
    - Duns & Bradstreet (dnb.com)
    - Vault (vault.com)
    - Corporate Information (corporateinformation.com).

  Most are free services but require registration. Some of the more
  extensive databases require membership.
- Use a social networking website. Linkedin (linkedin.com) is the best one of the bunch but you can sometimes find individual profiles on Facebook simply by putting the company name into the search function.
- Call the office receptionist/operator and ask who'd be responsible for reviewing sponsorship proposals.
- Google the company and the position. Never underestimate the power of search engines and public information.
- If you have a name but no contact information for the person, try variations of their name/position in an email to the company. For example, if their name is "Jacob Smith" and they are the VP of marketing at the Wedge company, then email "jacobsmith@wedgeco.com" in the "to" field. In the "BCC" field, add all variations of the name (such as jacobs@wedgeco.com, jsmith@wedgeco.com, marketing@wedgeco.com, etc.). This way, it won't be appear that you are sending spam (filters catch the addresses in the

"to" field but not "bcc") and that you have a more direct link to that person.

Don't Start with the Sponsorship Packet

Whatever you do, don't make the initial contact a mailed physical packet. Always begin with some kind of direct connection so you know who to contact. As permission to follow-up after sending them the packet and ask for an appointment a few days later to review the information.

6 THE SPONSORSHIP PROPOSAL OUTLINE

When you are ready to send your sponsorship proposal, you'll want to impress the prospect with something that is professional, well researched, creative, and highlights why working with you is a huge opportunity for them. Remember, the key is to target a few, well-matched prospects rather than spamming a multitude of companies for potential support. The more that you can invest into demonstrating a good match for their target audience, the better. Finally, review every page of the proposal and answer this: does it make someone want to be involved or is it just extraneous information that is not relevant to either brand?

Presentation Format, Optimum Content and Length

Here's a general outline/template that you can adapt to be more effective in your sponsorship packet. You should design your packet specifically for print as well as a digital file. The most important thing to keep in mind is the perspective of the sponsor: How does the proposal benefit them/their customers/their employees? What can you offer that is different than the other sponsorship proposals being sent to them? Is it easy to take action?

The Format:

1. **Cover** - Make it distinctive. You might consider adding something like "2012 Sponsorship Proposal Prepared

Especially For [the company]" with their logo on it. Give them plenty of opportunities to visualize working with you.

2. **The Call Out (optional):** The second page can be for a large dramatic image/photo or some of the major "bragging rights" stats. Artists can typically use this page as the "one sheet" - a one page descriptor of who you are, major stats or accomplishments, or press excerpts/testimonials from other sponsors.

3. **The Partnership:** This is where you want to focus on the main benefits for working with your organization. What are the main ways you and the sponsor are a good fit?

4. **The Fact Sheet:** The nitty-gritty details of your event, tour, or organization that they are sponsoring. Cover all of the major who/what/when/where/why questions, such as as "What is the event?," "Where does the event take place?," "Who is involved?," "Why should I be sponsoring this event," etc.

5. **Key Marketing Information:** This is where your research into your industry pays off. You'll want to talk about your niche market, the demographics of your audience (and who you are targeting), how you will be messaging your brand/event along with their company, and talk about successes with past sponsorship campaigns.

6. **Co-Branded Marketing Opportunities:** You'll want to send 3-6 custom, creative pitches to the company that allows for them to visualize working with you. This should play directly off of your niche market/their target audience. The more custom the idea, the higher the asking price that you can fetch. It also helps you stand out from other sponsorship opportunities that only offer logo placement. Marketing folks love creative ways to showcase their brand, especially to an interested audience who they might never be able to reach in any other way. If there is also a "viral" component to one of the ideas, that's even better.

7. **The Benefit List:** List all of the benefits that the company gets from sponsoring you. Put your emphasis on the more custom, creative options and less on the generic commodities that typical sponsorship packages offer (such as logo placement). This is your formal offer so make it as clear as possible on what they can be expecting in return from their sponsorship dollars

or in-kind gifts. If you'll accept a payment schedule, include that as well.

8. **The Sponsorship Agreement:** The sponsorship agreement should be easy to complete and return. Details such as a self-addressed and stamped envelope are good. Add an extra bit of professionalism by having this portion printed on NCR (carbonless copy) paper where they can tear off a copy for themselves and send one to you. You can also do things such as adding a QR code or link to a digital version of the agreement.

Additional Tips on Your Sponsorship Packet

- **Sell benefits, not features:** Understand the difference between a direct sponsorship benefit and a feature. In sales, this was called "FAB selling," where you'd discuss the *feature* of product, how it provided an *advantage*, and what the direct *benefit* was to the consumer.

- **Focus on what is most relevant to the sponsor:** Every page should reinforce the notion that this is a good return on investment for the business. Don't just brag about how many attendees that you have at your event or how you make a difference in the community; explain how those things are all directly related to the success of the sponsorship program.

- **Don't appear needy:** People like to work with a program that is successful and professional. If they get the impression that you are needy, then they feel more like an underwriter for your expenses rather than a business partner. That isn't to say that you shouldn't be appreciative of their support, but how you present the opportunities does change the frame of mind in which they view your proposal.

- **Make it an easy sell:** Even if you have the vote of confidence of the marketing director or your point of contact, they probably have to get approval from a board, budget committee, supervisor, or stakeholders. Provide information that they can use to make it an easy sell internally to the decision makers.

- **Introduce confidence boosters:** If you have a great history running other sponsorship campaigns, share some of that success. Get testimonials from other business partners, who industry leaders who are already supporting you or involved with you. If sponsorship campaigns are new to your organization, then show a history of success or great media coverage of your events/activities/staff.

- **Offer a menu of options:** In addition to the more "custom" options, you can also offer a standard menu of options for those who are only interested in a tax write-off and not a full fledged co-branded marketing campaign.

- **Offer marketing solutions:** The more you can assist the marketing decisions of the campaign, the more likely they'll consider your campaign. If you can design and implement a successful marketing campaign with a higher return on investment than what they'd ordinarily spend on other marketing efforts, then the decision to go with you is a no brainer. If sponsoring you seems like it will require a lot of hand-holding or follow up on their part, it only sounds like extra work that they don't need to be doing.

- **Pricing Structure:** The price points should provide a good value for what you are offering. The benefits you are selling for your niche audience should reflect that. How many people will you reach (impressions)? How much of a connection back to their business are you providing for the money?

- **Make it as long as it needs to be:** You should make every effort to keep the overall packet as concise as possible, which is why whenever I am asked about length, I just say to keep it as long as it needs to be…no more, no less. However, if you are looking for a hard and fast number, just try and keep it around 4 – 12 pages (it depends on what you're proposing.

7 THE SHOTGUN SPONSORSHIP

When Demand is High and You have an Immediate Deadline

Let's just face it. Most non-profit organizations, bands, athletes, etc. are busy and don't have the time/resources to dedicate to the pursuit of sponsorships as often as we'd like. There are some situations where you don't need a customized, full-on partnership. There are times where you just need some quick, simple donations for your event. This includes silent auctions and other similar fundraising efforts (such as a wine wall) or a blanket campaign where you don't have specific objectives to meet.

Here's how to launch a successful shotgun approach:

1. **Get a database or list of potential sponsors** separated out by industry. For example, you can have a list of bookstores, wineries, theme parks, clothing companies, etc. The reason why you want to segment by industry is because there should be a specific ask that is relevant to what they're able to offer.
2. **Create one basic "ask" email** that is 2-3 paragraphs covering who you are, what your cause is, what you are looking for them to donate (such as books, bottles of wine, or silent auction items).
3. **List the major benefits** for their donation (recognition at the event with high-profile attendees, business card with donation, in program thank you list, etc.) and explain how their donation will be used (sold in silent auction, given to volunteers, etc.).

4. **An easy call to action** should also be included, such as an address of where they can mail the items or who to contact so that a pickup can be arranged. If you have a deadline on when you need the answer, include that as well.
5. **Send one email to yourself, BCC the rest of the contacts.** Do not send an email with hundreds of recipients in the "to" field. That's just tacky and can trigger spam filters.
6. **Repeat the process over again with the next category.**

The key with this campaign is to send emails to as many contacts as possible and hope that a certain percentage of recipients will want to make a small, easy donation to your campaign. There's no big funding with this and you want to cover as much ground as possible.

Some helpful tips when using the shotgun approach:

- **Search for collections of information:** There are many websites that list specific vendors or contacts by industry and area. For instance, you can easily find wineries by state or region because there are huge databases for them. Even if you don't find a website listing them, you can use a tool such as Google Maps to find a listing (and then do further searching for the business contact info).
- **Spend more time on what will give you the biggest return:** If you have an event that is catered around a theme or need, use your time focusing on sponsors that speak to that need first.
- **Follow up with a phone call:** After sending the email, wait 72 hours and follow up with each contact by calling them directly. This gives them time to review your email and also adds a personal touch.
- **Create your own database:** As you search for contacts, build up a sponsorship database by creating a spreadsheet with the business name, address, phone, fax, website, and email address in separate fields. This will save time in the long run because you can just copy and paste all of the addresses in the "email" column in one message. If they have an online contact form instead of a direct email address, put that into a different column altogether - it will save you time on the back end.

- **Get help:** Collecting email addresses is something that anyone can do. Ask for some volunteers or friends who are willing to donate some time to help with this task.
- **Highlight the business connection:** You'll still want to highlight some of the benefits of donating for their business if you can, such as reaching a specific target audience, tax deduction, recognition of their gifts, etc.
- **Always follow up:** Whenever anyone replies to you (even if they decline), give a personal reply thanking them for their time or willingness to help. Always take the time to be courteous, you never know if they change their mind or want to help in the future.
- **Think shotgun, not laser:** For this type of campaign, it is all about the numbers. You want to send your message out to as many people as possible, hoping it sticks.

8 HOW TO FOLLOW UP THE RIGHT WAY

Developing a Partnership

Treat all of your sponsors as a business partner. Talk to them about the process, what they'd like to see out of the campaign and how you can help them strengthen their brand. In addition to creating the partnership with them, you will need to effectively measure sponsorship outcomes so that you can both evaluate the return on investment in the campaign.

Proof of Performance

Sponsorship reports are often referred to as "proof of performance." Deliver any co-branded materials to them such as brochures, t-shirts, posters, website URL's, etc. as a way to say thank you as well as to demonstrate the deliverables of the sponsorship campaign. In addition, send them detailed analytics that they can include in their own evaluations. This include: website statistics (traffic data, amount of time spent, locations of users), social media analytics (including growth on the sponsor's pages if you have access to that), attendance of your events, and any other relevant data. If the sponsorship is spread over time, send them regular updates throughout the partnership period. For instance, it would be appropriate to send quarterly updates with an annual review for a campaign that lasts one year. You want to show that not only did you deliver on your promises, but that you exceeded their expectations.

Many companies still rely on traditional sponsorship measurement approaches. In television coverage, this includes a second-by-second tally of focused logo exposure. In print media, this is measured by the actual square inches in an ad or the amount of columns an article on the brand may take up. Using estimated formulas, this calculated into an approximate retail dollar value (how much an equivalent ad would cost). While there are several companies that do these measurements for hire (and now include new media like internet coverage), it can be quite expensive so it isn't worthwhile unless you had dedicated public information personnel who needed to do this anyway. If you do want to get information about media coverage or sponsorship reports, look into Cision Point (cisionpoint.com), Joyce Julius (joycejulius.com) or similar "listening" services.

Finally, the reality is that there is no exact equivalent for sponsorship measurements. For example, a 30 second-advertising message that sells a brand's products or services is not going to produce the same results as 30 seconds of coverage linking the brand to a deeply meaningful community cause or an endorsement from a rock band with an extremely enthusiastic fan base. There have been several well-researched studies measuring sponsorship outcomes (cognitive study, affective outcomes, behavioral, and so on) and they all show positive results in linking a sponsor brand with a well-matched sponsor recipient. For more information, please see *Sponsorship-Linked Marketing: Opening the Black Box* by Cornwell, Weeks, and Roy, *Journal of Advertising:* Summer 2005.

The overwhelming majority of sponsors will not be looking for detailed case studies or even retail dollar outcomes. Most sponsors just want to get some kind of information to justify the investment into your cause. If you can prove that you brought better results than if they bought a weekly ad in the paper, you're already ahead of the game. Remember, the sponsorship manager or marketing director usually has to justify the expenses and will have to share the findings with a board or committee at the end of the year. Certainly, the more information that you give them showing a return on investment, the more compelling it will be for them to continue or increase their sponsorship. **The bottom line: always over deliver your promises.**

Here's how you present proof of performance:

- **The major statistics:** Give detailed information that shows the number of website hits (Google Analytics has excellent tools they would be interested in such as the amount of time spent on the site, search queries, demographics, etc.), social media analytics, and coverage in all forms of media.
- **Audience information:** Remember, the key is to demonstrate that you are constantly in touch with the niche market that the sponsor is trying to reach. If you have the available information (mostly available through social media analytics), show the type of fans who have been following you online, watching your videos (especially one where the sponsor is featured), or any media that caters to a specific audience. You might also consider getting statistics about that media source's audience (circulation, demographics, etc.) which is usually available in their advertising information section.
- **The hard proof:** Give the sponsor a copy of anything that you printed or had made that has their name on it. If it is a promotional item or merchandise, give several to for their employees or the key staff that were involved in helping make the sponsorship happen.
- **Consistency:** If you have a long term partnership or campaign, deliver summarized information on a regular basis so that they know how the sponsorship is performing.
- **Brand connection:** Anytime your audience thanks you for recommending the sponsor's products and services or a new customer is made from the relationship, collect that information to include when you deliver your report.

The Personal Touch

Go the extra mile when it comes to thanking the sponsor for their support. Don't just send a thank you card or email, but give them something meaningful that they can keep and positively reflect on the experience of working with you. If you're a non-profit organization, perhaps a thank you note from one of your constituents would be appropriate. If you are an artist, include signed merchandise. After a major tour in 2010, I hand-delivered an autographed drum cymbal that we broke mid-tour to our presenting sponsor that is still hanging up in their office today. For our other high-level sponsors, I sent thank you cards, gift cards to a favorite restaurant, photos, and merchandise.

Not all decisions are made specifically from a business point of view. A sponsor is going to be financially as well as personally invested into your cause, so create some personal touches to your communication to strengthen your partnership with them. That's how you create lifelong supporters.

For an example of a proof of performance report, see Appendix D.

APPENDIX A: EMAIL TEMPLATES

Email Template for the Touring Band: The Generic Ask

This is a general template that I shared on my music industry blog (www.laststopbooking.com) that artists could adapt to begin communication with potential sponsors. In fact, this is nearly the same email that I have used to successfully connect with thirteen of my current sponsors for my band, The Slants. Simply fill in your information and send (be sure to get a direct contact if possible). Send this one message at a time, never BCC multiple contacts or companies (such as in the Shotgun Approach as covered earlier).

Dear [contact name],

My name is [your name] and I manage the band [band name]. We are [elevator pitch here]. I am contacting you today because I would like to schedule a time where we can talk about doing some cross promotion through a partnership.

Since [start date, we have toured the country [x] times, released [x] albums, and have been featured in press such as [x,y,z]. We typically book venues in the [x] capacity range with a draw of [x]. Through the years, we've collected over [x] contacts on our mailing list and social media websites combined. With our [upcoming tour schedule or new album], we can give you company great promotion through efforts such as [your best co-branded marketing campaign idea here].

We are looking to build a long-term relationship that will benefit all parties involved. With other partners such as [sponsors/endorsements], we can provide great referrals regarding the return on investment you will receive from working with [band name].

[List website + Social Media Sites or EPK here]

I look forward to your prompt response and would love to discuss details further by email or phone. What other information can I provide to further this discussion?

Sincerely,
[your name]
[your phone]
[your email]

Email Template for the Touring Band: Specific Campaign

If you have a specific ask, this would be a better fit because it is more direct and can be catered specifically towards the sponsor:

Dear [contact name],

My name is [your name] and I manage the band [band name]. We are [elevator pitch here]. I am contacting you today because I would like to schedule a time where we can talk about doing some cross promotion through a partnership.

Our band has been especially successful working with this a target audience of [insert niche market here] and we perform for [x number] fans every year throughout [target area]. I know you've been looking to grow your business in this area and I'd like to talk about specific ways to reach this audience for you. One idea is [best specific partnership idea here].

We've worked with companies such as [x,y,z] and have a track record of success. If you're able to provide just 15 minutes of your time, I'd love the opportunity to go over this idea in more detail. When would be a good time to schedule a call or meeting?

Sincerely,
[your name]
[band/your contact information/websites]

Email Example for a Specific Ask with a Deadline

This is an example of an actual email I sent in 2010 to get some donations on an extremely tight deadline. Our band was shooting a music video and we realized that some major props were missing so I began contacting custom providers one week before we began filming. Not only was I able to get them shipped overnight from an international supplier, but we made some new friends who are also very involved in one of our main niche markets: the anime convention industry.

Hi,

My name is Simon Tam. I manage Asian dance rock band, The Slants.

The Slants are the only all-Asian American synth-pop/dance rock band in the United States and are known for widely playing anime conventions, Asian festivals, and rock clubs throughout the world. They've won multiple "Album of the Year" awards, have been featured on over 1200 radio stations, tv shows, magazines, and websites including "All Things Considered" on the NPR network and being on the "Hot List" of the late Shojo Beat magazine.

I wanted to get in touch with you because we are beginning production on a music video next week (09/03/10) for the song "How the Wicked Live," which you can hear at theslants.com

The music video is going to be an homage to the film Battle Royale, with members of the band taken to a desolate factory to kill each other off. While we might be experts in music and promotion, no one on our team has costume making talent. That's why I wanted to contact you about the Battle Royale collars that you have for sale on your website.

I wanted to see if you'd be willing to donate four of your collars for the music video. In exchange, you would get full credits for the BR collars (in the music video credits). We will also promote your website to our mailing list of over 30,000 contacts (most are anime convention fans or industry). The music video will be played at anime conventions across the planet. It will also be promoted with our publicist (In Music We Trust) and screened for spin.com, VH1, MTV2, Myspace Music, and other national media. Of course, you will also receive copies of The Slants' materials including all three albums and copies of the music video on DVD. There would be great promotional opportunities for you both and inside of the anime convention industry.

Is this something that you would be able to donate?

Because we are beginning production next Friday, we would need the four collars immediately. Please let me know by Monday, August 30 if you will be able to agree to these terms. If you'd like to get more information on the band, you can visit the sites below. You can also call me at any time.

Regards,
Simon Tam
[contact info/band websites]

P.S: For a partial listing of anime conventions The Slants have appeared at, you can visit: [link here]

Email Template for the Non-Profit Fundraising Event (direct relationship)

This type of email is one that I have used multiple times to get support from personal or professional connections made while working in the non-profit world. Personalize it with your "voice" and your cause. The main point of this email is to further the conversation; if you already have a solid relationship, just call them and ask for a lunch meeting to talk more about your fundraising event.

Dear [contact name]

This is [your name], from [organization name here]. It was great seeing you at the Chamber of Commerce event last week [or other recent contact].

I wanted to get in touch with you because I was thinking about our organization's [upcoming event name] and how your business would make a great fit. As you might know, we work directly with [niche audience] and its' the kind of audience you've been trying to reach for some time now.

I would love to talk to you more about a partnership where we can work together to expand your business in this community. Some of the ideas that come to mind include [1-2 creative partnership ideas] but I'd love to meet for coffee and talk about other ways we can work together.

When would be a good time to schedule a call or meeting? is there any other information can I send you?

Sincerely,
[your name]
[your phone]
[your email]
[event website]

45

Email Template for anyone with a mutual contact

If you're able to, try and have a mutual contact make the introductory email, or better yet, a face-to-face meeting. However, if that person is reluctant or busy, then ask for permission to use their name when contacting the sponsorship prospect. This is one example of how you can do that.

Dear [contact name]

This is [your name], from [organization name here]. We are [elevator pitch here]

[mutual contact] suggested that you might be interested in growing your audience in the [specific data] area and that we'd be able to help you out. As you might know, we work directly with [niche audience] through our annual event, [event name].

I would love to talk to you more about a partnership where we can work together to expand your business in this community. Some of the ideas that come to mind include [1-2 creative partnership ideas] but I'd love to meet for coffee and talk about other ways we can work together.

When would be a good time to schedule a call or meeting? is there any other information can I send you?

Sincerely,
[your name]
[your phone]
[your email]
[event website]

Email Template for Shotgun Campaign (wine for silent auction)

Please go through my notes under "Shotgun Approach" on how to effectively use this method. You can easily substitute out the wine for any product; a specific, direct, and quick ask is the main objective here.

To Whom it May Concern:

This is [your name], from [organization name here]. [elevator pitch here].

I'm contacting you in regards to our annual fundraising event, [event name]. This year's event is being held on [date] at [location]. We are expecting [x number] attendees, which includes [target audience]. We are looking for bottles of wine for our silent auction and are hoping that you can help.

Are you able to donate a few bottles of wine, including any excess, sample bottles, or back stock? We will be recognizing all gifts in this year's program as well as in a live, rotating slide-show that will include your winery's logo. Any size donation would be appreciated and is fully tax deductible.

I would be more than happy to arrange a time for pick up and will be calling in a few days to follow up. Thank you so much for your time and for supporting the cause.

Sincerely,
[your name]
[your phone]
[your email]
[event website]

APPENDIX B: SPONSORSHIP PACKET EXAMPLE: MUSIC ARTIST

This first example of a sponsorship packet is one that I created for The Slants in 2011. It's a highly stylized, almost like a magazine or comic book since the target audience of the band fell in the world of anime conventions and anime fans. Again, the content, layout, and even the dollar ranges that you use for your proposal should be entirely up to you and what you think makes the most sense for your brand. This example is to show you how you can get creative with the layout, highlight key information, and inject branding into the process. If you'd like a copy of the file (since it is originally formatted for 8.5x11, just get in touch with me and I'll be happy to email you a copy).

The cover, made to look like the cover of a magazine. The bar code on the bottom left is from one of our albums, though you might want to include a QR code that leads to a copy of your sponsorship packet online (or website).

[Letter From the Editor]

In 2007, The Slants kicked off their career in a small dive bar in Portland, OR. Three years later, we could barely believe what we achieved in that short time: ten tours across North America, released three albums, we rejected a million dollar recording contract, and performed at more anime conventions than any other band in existence. However, the greatest barometer of success has been the feedback of the fans and the people we've worked with. What an incredible journey!

Sure, the band has a track record of success. With over 1,500 TV shows, radio stations, magazines, and websites talking about the group, it should be no surprise how many results you get when doing an online search of "The Slants." But the best reason to work with us is that we're easy to work with. You'll get unexpected results, innovative ideas for getting your products and services to new audiences, and get great return for your investment.

You'll get genuine, viral, influential exposure that buying ads can't even come close to!

If you have any questions, contact me anytime.

Regards,
Simon Tam
theslants@theslants.com

Contact Info:

The Slants LLC
8026 SE Reedway St
Portland, OR 97206
(226) 24-SLANT

Management:
Last Stop Booking Agency
Simon@laststopbooking.com

Publicity:
In Music We Trust PR
Alex@inmusicwetrust.com
(503) 557-9661

Official Websites:
theslants.com
myspace.com/theslants
facebook.com/theslants
twitter.com/theslants
youtube.com/slantsvideos

Continuing on the magazine theme, the introductory letter is formatted in the same way. I always try to offer a personal element to this, especially since I only send the packet out after I've made personal contact with the sponsorship prospect.

10 REASONS TO SPONSOR THE SLANTS FOR THIS YEAR

Reach the Asia American Market.
Asian Americans are the second fastest growing population in the U.S. It's a wide open audience that is extremely loyal to brands.

The Young Adult Audience.
Nearly 70% of the band's fan base lies in the 18-34 age range.

Opt-In Lists
Our fans aren't bombarded with ads or friend requests. They take the time to follow the band by choosing to opt-in and subscribe to our mailing lists, social networking websites, and updates. You'll have a ready and willing audience.

Innovation Invasion!
We pride ourselves on coming up with unique, co-branded opportunities that make sense for your products and our audiences.

Huge Publicity Attention
In the last 3 years, The Slants have had access to a listening/reading audience of over 25 million people from radio, press, and televised features.

Huge Investment Potential
The Asian American and youth market comprise over $1 trillion in annual spending.

Helping the Community
In the past 3 years, The Slants have helped raised over $500,000 for charitable organizations around the world.

Genuine Marketing
We only align ourselves with products and services that we truly appreciate. Our genuine candor definitely shows with our endorsements of partner companies.

In-Person Exposure
Not only do The Slants have a strong online presence, but with a regular national touring schedule, they bring your brand to audiences across North America on a regular basis as well.

You'll Be More Cool
The Willamette Week states that "No other band in Portland has cultivated its image quite as well as synthy dance-pop quarter The Slants." The Slants have a unique charm and personality that endears fans like no other band does today.

FACTS, NUMBERS, & THINGS FOR YOUR CONSIDERATION...

- 1.7 Million hits at theslants.com since 2008
- In the first 3 years: 10 tours, 3 albums, and 300 live appearances across the globe.
- Featured on 1,500+ radio stations. TV shows, magazines, and websites worldwide.
- "Album of the Year" from the Portland Music Awards, Rockwired Magazine, Willamette Week, Shojo Beat, AsiaXpress, and many more.
- First and only Asian band to be a Fender Music spotlight artist, worldwide.
- Over 20 sponsors and endorsements from industry leaders around the world.

"They've described themselves as 'Chinatown Dance Rock' but The Slants are far from a novelty act. The band's infectious, urgent electro-pop has won fans of all stripes and colors, from anime aficionados to comic collectors to musos and beyond, and their rollicking live show is not to be missed"
(*The Stranger*, Vol 17, No 15)

Always try and put the major statistics, facts, and dramatic information of interest in the beginning. You want to grab their attention as soon as possible so that they know they're working with a professional, reliable brand that has a history of success.

"The Asian Band That Could..."
The Slants, a history

It's rare for a band to be headlining shows with 5,000-15,000 fans in attendance and internationally touring in their first year as a band. Perla Cadena of Sony BMG Music Ent. says "They are setting new records everyday for what an independent artist can accomplish."

What originated as a side project for Simon Young in 2007 proved to be one of the most energetic and contagious movements of music in our time. Incase you haven't heard, The Slants are the first and only all Asian American synth-pop band in the world and they have been melting faces off all over the globe.

Kicking off the band's career at a tiny dive bar in Portland, OR, The Slants soon found themselves on tour and in demand worldwide performing at music halls, colleges, and anime conventions. Within months, they released their debut album *Slanted Eyes, Slanted Hearts*, winning multiple awards from the likes of Willamette Week, Rockwired, AsiaXpress, and the Portland Music Awards. Since that first iconic show in 2007, The Slants have been cited as the "Hardest Working Asian American Band" (slanteyefortheroundeye.com), toured North America ten times, rejected a million dollar recording contract, were the first and only Asian band to be a Fender Music artist, and according to U.S Congress, the first rock band to play inside a state library.

"Hardest Working Asian American Band"
(slanteyefortheroundeye.com)

The Willamette Week summarizes the band's history perfectly: "It's a great story: All-Asian synthcore troupe lands anime festival, achieves instantaneous notoriety from over packed fireball-laden maelstrom, inspires John Woo and Dragon Ball Z fans toward aggro electro and—just months after its first practice—books gigs across the globe. As shadow warriory as the Slants' rise has been, it's still all about the tunes, and the band's debut floor-filling synth pop bristling with all the menace and grandeur of its oft name checked cultural icons - is propulsive, cinematic and impossible to ignore."

By the end of 2008, the band had been featured in over 1,200 magazines, radio stations, websites, and television shows for their self-proclaimed "Chinatown Dance Rock," including a feature on NPR's "All Things Considered" that blasted across 700 FM stations across the country for months.

The following year, The Slants headlined a SXSW showcase (other acts at the festival included Katy Perry, Metallica, and Devo), launched several more tours spanning North America, and released a dance remix album entitled *Slants! Slants! Revolution*, while donating 100% of the proceeds to benefit cancer research affecting Asian American women.

2010 saw the release of The Slants' third album, *Pageantry*. *Pageantry* featured a number of music icons including Cory Gray (The Decemberists) and Brandon Eggleston (Modest Mouse), The harder hitting, guitar driven songs still featured The Slants' signature dance rock flavor and again, massive touring throughout the country continued.

The Slants have shared the stage with acts such as Apl.de.Ap (Black Eyed Peas), Vampire Weekend, Girl Talk, Girugamesh, M.O.V.E and Boom Boom Satellites. And now they're ready to perform at your event.

The band's biography, written specifically with the sponsorship prospect in mind.

Editor's Choice and Featured In:

- *Asian Week*: The largest English printed Asian newspaper in the world
- IGN.com: The most popular video game site online.
- *Shojo Beat*: The largest shojo magazine in North America.
- Other anime magazines such as *Protoculture Addicts*, *Anime Food*, *Manga Café*, and more
- Las Vegas Weekly (front cover), Space Shower TV (Japan), LA Weekly, City Beat, Comcast/Xfinity, SF Gate, and thousands more!

The Slants have been Guests of Honor at:

Anime Banzai (2010)
Texas Rockfest (2010)
Anime Oasis (2007-2010)
Kamikazecon (2010)
Sakuracon (2008/2009)
Animethon (2009)
Ikkicon (2009)
RealmsCon (2009)
Anime Central (2009)
SXSW (2009)
Nan Desu Kan (2008)
Kumoricon (2007/2008)
MTAC Infinity
MTAC Ninja
PortConMaine (2008)
Anime Evolution (2008)
Tokyo in Tulsa (2008)
Pacific Media Expo (2007)
SacAnime (2008/2010)
No Brand Con (2008)
Yaoi Jamboree (2008)
Persacon (2008)
Aki-Con (2008)
Animix (2008)
New England Fan Expo 08
MewCon (2009)
Mizuumi-Con
Asian Street Heritage Fair
Dragon Moon Festival
Portland Erotic Ball
...and many more!

The juicy gossip:
WHAT OTHERS ARE SAYING ABOUT
THE SLANTS

TESTIMONIALS FROM THE ANIME/CULTURE CONVENTION INDUSTRY:

"I've been working cons since 2003 on an executive level and I have to say that **pound for pound, dollar for dollar, The Slants are the best value and guests that any convention can bring in, anywhere**. They work harder than anyone else, have a huge strong base, fans love them, and they're joy to work with."
John Krall
Sakuracon: Con Chair, Director of Programming
Kumoricon: Guest Relations, Director of Programming

"**The Slants are easily one of the best bands an Asian pop culture or Asian cultural convention could benefit from**. They ignite a fierce passion for Asian culture through their edgy, pulsating electro-rock sound, and their energy level envelopes the entire audience."
Sarah Edge
JRock Events USA

"The Slants hit the stage...the **performance was energetic** and it was clear that the crowd found it easy to get into"
Jrock Revolution

"The Slants have an edgy-yet-fun Asian aesthetic that fits in perfectly with Shojo Beat's J-Pop-centric demographic—many of our fans are already familiar with them through their performances at various manga and anime-related shows and conventions. Plus, in collaborating with the band on editorial coverage and two contest promotions, **we've all found The Slants to be creative, motivated, and easy to work with**. We look forward to future opportunities with The Slants."
Megan Bates
Senior Editor for Shojo Beat & Viz Media

"The Slants were a pleasure to work with. **They're the most professional band I've ever booked** for my show. **They showed up early & communication was a breeze**. No surprises. Plus, the fans loved them. I'd definitely book them again."
Dan Houck
SacAnime: Con Chair

They astounded me so much with their darkly haunting "Chinatown Dance Rock" at the Pacific Media Expo, that I knew I had to confront them! It came as no surprise that the **J-rock fans were mesmerized by the Slants' charm and intensity proving they are very appropriate for the US J-rock and anime convention circuit.**"
Marty Shane
President, Pacifiction Records

WHAT SOME OF THE PRESS ARE SAYING:

"No longer is Japan, China and Korea the only places housing quality Asian rock bands! Welcome to The Slants. A US-based rock/synth/electro band that frequents popular anime and manga conventions...did I mention that one of them knows how to breathe fire?"
IGN.com (Anime Special Report)

"The Slants are easily one of the best bands I've ever seen."
Backbeat Online

"The band started playing at various anime and manga conventions, where they drew their first wave of fans; their songs about alienation, solidarity, and Asian-American identity hit a nerve with audiences. In fact, everything about The Slants, from their name to their lyrics, seems aimed at debunking what it means to be different or strange. "
Static Multimedia

"They kick some serious ass...this band knows what it's doing"
angryasianman.com

No other band in Portland has cultivated its image quite as well as synthy dance-pop quartet the Slants. Pageantry, the band's latest album, advances the group's mystique, with a healthy jolt of hard rock that further proves the Slants' mass appeal and staying power.
The Willamette Week

Demonstrating press coverage and providing testimonials from others that we've worked with establishes credibility. In this example, it's to specifically show credibility in the anime, video game, and comic industry.

FAQs
about
sponsoring
THE SLANTS

What makes The Slants different than any other band?

The Slants are the first and only all-Asian American dance rock band in the world. Not only do they have a unique audience, but they're heavily involved with their fans with exceptionally strong ties.

How often does the band play? How much exposure will I get?

The band spends an average of six to eight weeks per year touring (sometimes spread by extended weekends) with bi-weekly performances in the Northwest region. Every year, the band is involved with Asian cultural events with a cumulative audience of over 500,000. In addition, The band updates their social networking sites at least three times per day. The amount of exposure you'll receive is proportionate to your own involvement and investment with the band. We are always happy to take promotional materials to distribute while on tour or to come up with other ideas to get you more exposure.

Where is the music of the band available?

We have international distribution through Burnside Distribution Company and our albums are available with over 256 different online retailers and 15,000 stores worldwide.

The band also has several licensing agents who work to have the band's music placed with clients such as HBO, Fox, CBS, ABC, and major motion pictures.

What're some other acts that you've played with?

We've performed at events with Apl.de.Ap (Black Eyed Peas), Katy Perry, Metallica, Devo, Girugamesh, M.O.V.E, Boom Boom Satellites, Ketchup Mania, Smile DK, Melt Banana, Cheap Trick, Peelander Z, B.O.B, Passion Pit, PJ Harvey and many more.

How will my company benefit from sponsoring your band?

You will be aligning your brand with one of the most active, resourceful, and respected artists in the world. Very few other independent bands receive the amount or quality of press that The Slants receive. Even fewer have the brand development, business know-how, and practical application of innovative marketing concepts that The Slants naturally grasp and implement.

As a supporter, you'll also get quarterly updates with behind the scenes information, such as website traffic reports, upcoming plans, amount of exposure your brand is receiving, and more.

How do I sign up?

Complete the attached form and send back to us. We can work out the details with you and come up with a customized plan that will make sense for everyone involved. There are multiple tiers that we offer, if you have any questions on what would be the best fit for you, then please don't hesitate to contact the band.

I always like to include a FAQ because it allows you to overcome objections before they are raised .It's just another format to present the information in a way that is concise, relevant, and easy to read.

54

Sponsorship Opportunities

Sponsorships are available as cash or in-kind production donation. In-kind donations will be considered for 50% of retail value, please contact for details. The term length of a sponsorship is one year.

PLATINUM SPONSOR (Presenting Sponsor): $5,000
- Tour naming rights (for any tour 10+ days in length during the year)
- Large, custom full color decal on tour trailer/vehicle (both sides)
- Logo on official tour poster and tour t-shirts
- Full page ad in official tour program
- Placement of advertising materials (postcards/brochures) on tour merch table
- Namesake mention on all press releases for tour (audience of approx. 15 million)
- Two free performances for corporate or outreach events
- Presentation opportunities at cultural/convention events
- Logo on 2011 tour stage banner
- Logo/presenting status on all tour video blog updates
- Premiere thank you on album linear notes
- Logo on theslants.com and myspace.com/theslants

GOLD SPONSOR (Title Sponsor): $3,000
- Large, custom full color decal on tour trailer/vehicle (both sides)
- Logo on tour poster and t-shirts
- 1/2 Page ad in official tour program
- Placement of advertising materials (postcards/brochures) on tour merch table
- One free performance for corporate or outreach event
- Special thanks on album linear notes
- Logo on theslants.com and myspace.com/theslants

SILVER SPONSOR: $1,500
- Small decals on tour trailer/vehicle (both sides)
- Small logo on tour poster
- Small logo on tour t-shirt
- 1/4 Page ad in official tour program
- Special thanks on album linear notes
- Logo on theslants.com and myspace.com/theslants

BRONZE SPONSOR: $750
- Small decals on tour trailer/vehicle (back only)
- Special thanks on album linear notes
- Logo on theslants.com and myspace.com/theslants

ENTRY SPONSOR (Community Support): $500
- Special thanks on album linear notes
- Logo on theslants.com and myspace.com/theslants

A typical sponsorship proposal based on "sponsorship levels." You can get creative with the levels, they don't have to be limited to types of metals (you can always add a personal touch by branding the sponsorship levels as well). Always start with the top and work your way down. Offer some tangible, creative options that build a real sense of value.

<u>Sponsorship Agreement</u>

Company/Organization name: _____

Contact Name: _____ Position: _____

Email: _____ Phone: (_____) _____

Address: _____

_____

Company URL: _____

Sponsorship Level (select one):
___ Platinum ($5,000)
___ Gold ($3,000)
___ Silver ($1,500)
___ Bronze ($750)
___ Entry ($500)

Additional Product Support That You Would Like to Provide:

_____

_____

Other Co-Branded Marketing Opportunities That You'd Like Considered:

_____

_____

_____

Total amount pledged: $_____

Signature: _____ Date: _____

Please return to:

For additional questions, contact Simon Tam   theslants@theslants.com

A typical sponsorship agreement.

APPENDIX C: SPONSORSHIP PACKET EXAMPLE: NON-PROFIT ORGANIZATION/EVENT

This is the San Diego Asian Film Foundation. They have one of the best event sponsorship packets that I've seen: it is clean, well-branded, and extremely effective. If you'd like more information on their organization, please visit www.sdaff.org

Simple cover page.

WHO WE ARE

The San Diego Asian Film Foundation (SDAFF) is a nonprofit organization that serves more than 40,000 people each year. Our mission is to **transform** and **connect** audiences with the human experience through the Pan Asian media arts. We strive to present meaningful programs that culturally connect, inspire and strengthen the community. Since 2000, we have served more than 200,000 people including independent artists, students, and the general public.

Through our Film Festival, Spring Showcase, Quarterly Screenings, Monthly Film Forums, Reel Voices Youth Documentary Program, and Digifest, we provide audiences in San Diego County and North America a cinematic window to the world.

An immediate introduction to the organization, the "Elevator Pitch."

OUR COMMITMENT TO YOU

As a sponsor, we are committed to crafting a meaningful partnership based on your marketing priorities and philanthropic values. We offer multiple platforms for brand exposure to a captured audience that generates memorable touchpoints. Previous corporate partners include:

SPONSORSHIP OPPORTUNITIES

FILM FESTIVAL   GALA AWARDS DINNER   SPRING SHOWCASE   YOUTH EDUCATION

2012 SDAFF SPONSORSHIP   5

Leading logos of big name sponsors right away gives credibility to the organization as well as the event. It says "we're professional and we attract professional businesses to partner with."

OUR AUDIENCE

The SDAFF attracts an often targeted by generally inaccessible audience of more than 40,000 highly influential brand, cultural and tech-savvy consumers of the creative class.

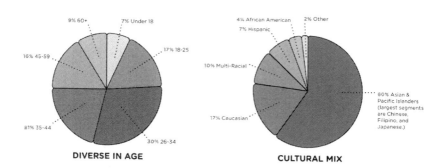

DIVERSE IN AGE

9% 60+
7% Under 18
17% 18-25
16% 45-59
21% 35-44
30% 26-34

CULTURAL MIX

4% African American
2% Other
7% Hispanic
10% Multi-Racial
60% Asian & Pacific Islanders (largest segments are Chinese, Filipino, and Japanese.)
17% Caucasian

Based on a survey of 5,000 attendees, the majority:

- Have individual income over $60,000/year with 20% above $100,000
- Have a college degree, graduate, or post-graduate degree
- Could identify sponsors and would prefer to do business with them

Asian Pacific Islander (API) Market Highlights

- APIs have the highest median household income of all groups in the U.S
- API purchasing power is estimated at $528 billion and is expected to grow to $752 billion by 2013*
- According to the Bureau of Labor Statistics, the average API household spends more than any other consumer household unit

*According to the Selig Center for Economic Growth from the University of Georgia's Terry College of Business

The demographic information here is more detailed than most sponsorship packets that you'll find. Right away, it shows who their target audience is and why that audience is a great fit for the potential sponsor.

MARKETING & MEDIA IMPRESSIONS

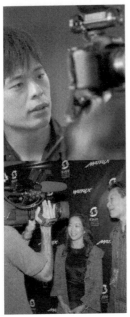

9 million plus media impressions in 2011

- **#1 Google Placement among all like Asian Film Festivals**
- **7,000+** fans on Facebook
- **4,000+** followers on Twitter
- **5,000+** eNewsletter subscribers
- **470,000+** views on SDAFF Youtube Channels
- **800+** Mobile SMS Subscribers
- **10,000+** readers on festival's Scribd.com page (social publishing site)
- **320,019** total website hits during month of the festival
- **100,566** Google Ad Words Impressions
- **600+** Sponsored Ads on Time Warner and Cox Cable
- **122** Sponsored TV Ads From NBC-Universal 7/39 San Diego
- **Major Media Partnerships** with DramaFever.com, NBC-UNI 7/39, The San Diego Union-Tribune, KPBS Radio, KoreAmJournal, Audrey Magazine, and MYX-TV.
- **Digifest 2011 (National)**
    - 5 million impressions through ads, banners, and pre-rolls
    - 14 million page views
    - 1 million unique visitors
    - 300,000 film views

Another great way to present the actual numbers of social media, media, and marketing impressions.

FILM FESTIVAL

The SDAFF is best known for its annual **ASIAN FILM FESTIVAL,** the largest film exhibition of Asian films on the West Coast. More than 20,000 people attend over the 9-day event in the Fall, which includes film premieres, live discussions with filmmakers, and numerous special events.

Depending on your budget, we offer venue naming rights, print and onscreen ads, video commercials, web and onsite banners, product sampling, collateral distribution, logo recognition, private receptions, tickets for clients/employees, speaking opportunities, and social media promotions.

Specific information on their signature event

$75,000	Title Sponsor (exclusive)	$15,000	Small Theater Sponsor
$50,000	Presenting Sponsor (exclusive)	$10,000	Festival Kick-off Sponsor
$25,000	Big Theater Sponsor (exclusive)	$7,500	Opening or Closing Night Sponsor
$15,000	Audience Award Sponsor (exclusive)	$7,500-15,000	Spotlight Sponsor
		$2,500-5,000	Community Sponsor
		$3,000	Free Films at Four Sponsor
		$2,500	Screening Sponsor
		$2,500	Youth Day

Additional customized packages available.
See Benefits Grid on page 12.

2012 SDAFF SPONSORSHIP   7

Sponsor tree chart (multiple options)

GALA AWARDS DINNER

Described as the "Asian American Oscars," the Gala Awards dinner is the highlight of the Film Festival where top films of the Festival are announced by celebrity presenters. More than 700 entertainment, business, and community leaders attend each year, offering an excellent platform for high-end clients.

$25,000	Presenting Sponsor
$10,000	Awards & Tributes Sponsor
$3,000	Wine Sponsor
$2,500	VIP Table

Additional customized packages available. See Benefits Grid on page 12.

Another event available for sponsorship opportunities with the organization.

Accuracy of Death

SPRING SHOWCASE

Celebrating Asian and Asian American films in this presentation of up to 10 programs to 5,000 attendees.

$10,000 Presenting Sponsor (exclusive)

$5,000 Special Events sponsor

$2,500 Screening Sponsor

Additional customized packages available. See Benefits Grid on page 12.

Another event available for sponsorship opportunities with the organization.

YOUTH EDUCATION

Since 2005, the SDAFF has transformed the lives of local youth through **REEL VOICES,** an intense documentary "boot-camp" teaching under-served high school students the art of digital storytelling. Student films premiere at the Festival then travel to other film festivals around the world. Many students pursue film school as a result of this program. Sponsorship opportunities range from $2,500 to $10,000.

ANGEL GATUS, REEL VOICES STUDENT
WINNER OF PBS'S PROJECT VOICESCAPE
AUDIENCE AWARD

ADAM LEE, REEL VOICES STUDENT
LOYOLA MARYMOUNT FILM STUDENT,
FULL SCHOLARSHIP

10   2012 SDAFF SPONSORSHIP

This includes general information about their work in the community.

For those only interested in advertising without additional sponsorship benefits

Video Commercial	$7,500
Onscreen Advertising	$2,000
Print Advertising	$500 (half page) $1,000 (full page)
Table	$200/day
Booth	$500/day

Booth and Advertising space is limited. To reserve space, email **advertising@sdaff.org**. Nonprofits receive 50% off above rates.

2012 SDAFF SPONSORSHIP 11

In addition to sponsorship options, brands have the opportunity to buy advertising through the organization as an alternative.

BENEFITS GRID

	Community ($2,500+)	Spotlight ($7,500+)	Gala Presenter ($25k)	Audience Award ($15k)	Theater Sponsors ($15-25k)	Presenting ($50k)	Title ($75k)	Spring Showcase Presenter
FESTIVAL PROGRAM BOOKLET								
Two Page Ad spread w/ preferred placement							X	
Full Page Color Ad - w/ preferred placement					LRG	X		
Full Page Color Ad				X	SMALL			
Full Page BW Ad								
1/2 Page Color Ad		X						
1/2 Page BW Ad			X					
Sponsor Page Logo Exposure		X	X	X	X	X	X	
External Insert	X						X	
MINI GUIDE								
Logo				X	X	X	X	X
Mini Advertisement							X	X
MARKETING								
Video Commercial			:30		LRG	:30	:60	:30
OnScreen Ad			X	X	X	X	X	X
Year-round presence on SDAFF homepage							X	
Seasonal ad on SDAFF homepage							X	X
Seasonal ad on Festival page		X		X	X	X		
Logo and link in Festival section		X	X	X	X		X	
Name and link in Festival section	X					X	X	
Spotlight in eNewsletter			X	X	X	X	X	X
Recognition on iPhone App					X	X	X	
Facebook Announcements (frequency TBD)			X		LRG	X	X	X
Twitter Announcements (frequency TBD)					LRG	X	X	X
Mailer insert			X		LRG	X	X	X
TICKETS								
All Access Pass			4	8	8	15	20	
Opening Night	2	5	4	5	5	10	15	
Closing Night	2	5	4	5	5	10	15	
General Comp Tickets	10	25	20	25	25	40	50	25
GALA								
Logo on Step & Repeat Banner			X				X	
Gala Table (10 seats) w/ VIP seating			X		X	X	X	
Gala Table (10 seats)		X		X				
Gala Seats	4							
Speaking/Presenting opportunity				X				
Logo Projection			X			X	X	
Company logo on Gala invite			X				X	
Verbal recognition			X				X	

**Benefits outlined in this grid can be customized based on budget and need

The benefits grid is another way to showcase the different sponsorship options available, the benefits received, and how they the different levels of sponsorship differ from one another.

APPENDIX D: PROOF OF PERFORMANCE EXAMPLE

This is an example of a typical proof of performance report that I send out after a sponsorship campaign. The more that it is personalized for the sponsor, the better. They want to know the specific details on how they are getting a return on investment for their brand. Show them. The example below was for a recent campaign I completed with a long time sponsor (names were removed for this publication).

THE SLANTS' TOUR WRAP UP:

Number of exclusive MP3 downloads with your brand featured : 8,250

During the tour, we personally handed out 5,000 postcards in 18 different states with our co-branding campaign. 16,542 miles were driven with your logos prominently displayed across our van and trailer.

Here's how we did online:

Exclusive tour video blog views: 4,413
Exclusive music video views: 6.854
Other music video views with prominent display of your brand: 146,281

Number of Visits to theslants.com with your logo featured (in 2011): 1,004,270

Number of countries receiving television broadcast of our videos: 81

Facebook activity:
Number of Followers: 12,690 (gain of 11,000+ during our campaign)
Increase in Post Views/Interactions (2011-2012): +658%
Increase in Post Feedback (2011-2012): +66%

YouTube activity:
Video Views: 284,046
Subscribers: 723

Myspace activity (past 90 days only)
Total Page Visits: 1,452
Total Song Plays: 3,334
Myspace Fans: 9,411

Monthly Email List:
Current Subscribers: 3,724
Unique Opens Rate: 16.6% Bounce Rate: 0.4%

Last.fm (online radio station)
Last.fm plays: 16,618
Last.fm subscribers: 1,062

Klout (measurement of influence online)
Klout Score: 61.2

Top 5 Topics The Slants are most influential about: music, video, [your brand], festival, sake

In addition to delivering this information, we provide at least one copy of every co-branded poster, banner, merchandise, etc. and an array of personal thank you cards from our staff, volunteers, and fans. Always over deliver!

ABOUT THE AUTHOR

Simon is best known as the founder of The Slants, the world's first and only all-Asian American dance rock band. Simon's unique approach to marketing and activism has been featured on NPR's "All Things Considered," Bloomberg News, USA Today, Comcast/XFINITY, Myx TV, Fuse TV, The Los Angeles Times, ELLE Magazine (Spain), Space Shower TV (Japan), and thousands more. His work has appeared in over 80 countries across six continents.

Simon has coordinated and appeared at over 1,200 events around the world, including major festivals such as SXSW, MusicFestNW, and the Asian Street Heritage Fair, both as a professional musician as well as a speaker. In 2012, Simon worked with the United States Department of Defense on "Operation Gratitude," a series of concerts to uplift the spirits of military stationed overseas during the holidays.

Simon also serves multiple non-profit organizations as a board member, leader, and volunteer. His marketing projects and volunteerism has earned several innovation and service awards.

You can find Simon's writing and current projects at: www.simontam.biz

27388810R00044

Made in the USA
Lexington, KY
09 November 2013